Original title:
Fragrant Musings

Copyright © 2025 Creative Arts Management OÜ
All rights reserved.

Author: Colin Leclair
ISBN HARDBACK: 978-1-80567-073-5
ISBN PAPERBACK: 978-1-80567-153-4

Hushed Blooms

In gardens where the daisies giggle,
They whisper secrets, oh so fickle.
The tulips tell jokes, a real delight,
While roses blush, not quite polite.

Sunflowers dance, they're quite the sight,
With wigs of pollen, in golden light.
A daffodil claims to know a prank,
While ivy just nods and gives a wink.

The Essence of Time

Time tiptoes softly, wearing clogs,
Tick-tock laughs from wise old frogs.
They leap through hours with a cheer,
While seconds bloom, oh dear, oh dear!

Each minute's a pie, quite the taste,
Where every crumb disappears in haste.
A clock, so grumpy, yells, 'Hurry up!',
But seconds just giggle, 'We're filling the cup!'

Perfumed Journeys

A sniffer dog dreams of scented trails,
Through fields of lavender, wagging tails.
He snouts around for that perfect whiff,
While petals toss snacks for a fragrant riff.

Bees buzz in tune, sharing sweet lore,
Of honey fountains and floral stores.
With every sip from blossoms wide,
The world smells funny, it's quite the ride!

The Breath of Spring

Spring's breath sneezes with pollen surprise,
While tulips disguise in colorful ties.
Butterflies flutter, all dressed up fine,
As grass gets crammed with a giggle divine.

The sun cracks jokes in its warming glow,
As raindrops dance, putting on quite a show.
With laughter sprouting from blooms so bright,
Spring's clever whispers tickle the night.

A Symphony of Fragrance

In a garden where the flowers bloom,
Bees buzz loudly, filling up the room.
A daisy plays a silly tune,
While roses giggle beneath the moon.

Lemon zest does a little jig,
While lavender prefers a small twig.
The marigold wears a funny hat,
While daisies dance around a fat cat.

Aromatic Journeys

Aromas waft from pots and pans,
Garlic smells like jazz in cans.
Onions cry in fragrant tears,
As spices laugh and switch their gears.

Cinnamon spins in a wild twirl,
Nutmeg flips and gives a whirl.
Together they take a bold ride,
In a pot where flavors collide.

The Dance of the Flowers

Daisies wear their polka dots,
Tulips strut, showing off their spots.
Sunflowers strike a silly pose,
While petunias giggle in soft prose.

Carnations twirl like they're at a ball,
While lilacs try not to fall.
In this garden, oh what glee,
The flowers dance, wild and free!

Whispers in the Air

The breeze carries tales of minty snacks,
While thyme tells stories of tasty hacks.
A hint of pepper sneezes loud,
As allspice skips and feels so proud.

Sage grins widely, sharing its tricks,
While basil twirls, pulling off some kicks.
In the air, laughter weaves and sways,
As spices frolic in joyful plays.

Bouquet of Hidden Thoughts

In the garden of giggles, I wander alone,
Sniffing the petals, a sweet overtone.
Laughter blooms wildly, as bees start to hum,
Whispers of jokes in the fresh springtime sun.

Daisies tease daisies, with stories to share,
Tulips all tickled, in their perfumed air.
Roses roll their eyes, in a blush of red,
While violets chuckle, 'You've got a big head!'

The Alchemy of Aroma

In the lab of the flowers, I mix up a brew,
A dash of old dandelion, and dreams that I knew.
Sunflower giggles as I stir in a smile,
The scent of a tickle, it takes but a while.

Feverfew fumes float in the air like a prank,
Basil bursts laughter, from its green, leafy tank.
With thyme on my side, oh what a delight,
I bottle up silliness, keep it for night.

Scented Echoes of Summer

In the heat of the day, the daisies all sway,
Chasing the sunshine, oh what a fun play.
Lilies leap joyfully, in skirts made of light,
While the vibrant blooms giggle, oh what a sight!

The cornflowers ponder, with shades oh so blue,
A breeze brings a chuckle, fresh laughter anew.
Petunias prance proudly, in rows side by side,
Spreading sweet scents that can't help but abide.

The Flower's Soft Embrace

In the garden of whimsy, each blossom has quirks,
Petals like giggles and soft, smiling smirks.
Sunshine spills laughter, the bees join the fun,
A meteor shower of whimsy's begun!

With each gentle rustle, the flowers engage,
They sway to the rhythm, a comical stage.
Marigolds chuckle, while daisies just dance,
In a soft, fragrant waltz, they twirl and prance.

The Songs of the Meadow

In the meadow, bees do hum,
As I trip over a flower's bum.
A daisy giggles, plucking my shoe,
'This dance is fun, what else will you do?'

Butterflies mimic my clumsy sway,
They giggle, these bugs, at my ballet.
A grasshopper joins, now it's a show,
What's next, a frog in a top hat? Oh no!

Perfumed Ponderings

The lavender whispers, 'What's that smell?'
Is it me or the room I fell?
A skunk rushes by, nose held high,
They claim it's a tease, I can't deny.

Daisies discuss the latest craze,
Are we stale, or just stuck in a haze?
Roses plot, with thorns for flair,
A scent battle's brewing, beware, beware!

Threads of Clarity

In my garden, I knit with care,
The mischief today? Hair everywhere!
A squirrel snags my yarn for a nest,
While I trip, calling, 'You're not the best!'

Tulips watch, with laughter so bright,
'Let's make a quilt — oh, what a sight!'
The wind steals my patterns, does a spin,
Now I'm weaving giggles with a cheeky grin.

Echoes of Blossoms

Petals whisper secrets, oh what fun!
'Did you hear what the daisies sung?'
A bumblebee takes a break for a laugh,
'We'll buzz like rockstars, get your autograph!'

Tulips sway, with flair they prance,
'Look at us, a blooming dance!'
A mockingbird joins, what a treat,
Together they create a silly beat.

The Allure of Freshness

A whiff of mint in the breeze,
Gives me chills, puts me at ease.
Fruits parade with scents so bright,
Bananas giggle, pure delight.

The garlic's charm, oh so bold,
Sends my taste buds into a fold.
Onions weep, yet they bring cheer,
Their pungent laughter we hold dear.

Seasons of Smell

Spring brings blooms with scents to spare,
Pollen dust in the springtime air.
Summer's heat makes roses sway,
While daisies giggle in the play.

Autumn's leaves, they swirl and dance,
As pumpkins plot their sweet romance.
Winter's chill brings scents so weird,
Hot cocoa dreams, oh how they steered.

Reverberating Petals

Petals whisper in soft tones,
Any snoring blooms need loans.
Daffodils with voices sing,
While sleepy tulips dream of spring.

Hibernating daisies yawn,
Until the sun brings raucous dawn.
Their perfume plots a great escape,
Through breezy fields, they're dressed in cape.

A Tryst with Nature

Bumblebees in a floral jam,
Creating chaos with a slam.
Butterflies flirt, they're on the prowl,
While daisies gossip with a growl.

A garlic herb in love's embrace,
Whispers sweet things with no trace.
Nature's joke, quite an affair,
Smells of laughter fill the air.

Essence of Stillness

In my garden, stillness grows,
With whispers soft, like tickled toes.
The daisies chuckle, the roses tease,
Even the grass hums, if you please.

The squirrels prance, a dance so bold,
Telling secrets in whispers old.
A statue smiles with frozen glee,
Who knew stillness could be so free?

Bees buzz about, their humor sweet,
Each bloom they visit, a merry treat.
Life's tranquil joke plays on repeat,
In this silent grove, we gossip discreet.

Yet, if silence had a sound,
It'd be laughter that knows no bound.
So here I sit with nature's cheer,
In essence of stillness, always near.

The Aroma of Dreams

I dreamt a dream of cake and pies,
With chocolate rivers and licorice skies.
Peanut butter clouds drift along,
While jellybeans sing a silly song.

The scents twist and twirl, a fragrant dance,
A perfume of jellybeans makes me prance.
With cinnamon breezes, I take a bite,
In this dreamland, everything feels right.

Pineapple fish swim through the air,
Lemonade rain, oh, what a flair!
Each waft a giggle, a chuckle, a wink,
In the aroma of dreams, I hardly think.

But wake me not from this candy scheme,
In the land of dreams, I reign supreme.
May the flavors linger, and surely gleam,
As I chase the sweet in every dream.

Perfumed Reflections

Mirror, mirror, on the wall,
What's that scent? Oh, do I smell?
Lavender in my hair today,
Or the leftover snacks from yesterday?

Reflections laugh, they twist and shout,
"Is that a whiff of burnt-out clout?"
A whir of mint or maybe cheese,
In this olfactory game, I'm hard to please.

A spritz of mystique, a dash of fun,
A cologne mishap? Just my luck, hon!
The shadows cha-cha with my toes,
Perfumed reflections, anything goes.

So here I stand, a scent delight,
In my own aroma, I take flight.
With every sniff, I find the glee,
In scented mischief, I am free.

Gardens of the Mind

In the garden where ideas bloom,
I plant a thought with all my room.
Watered with giggles and sunshine's gleam,
Watch them sprout into a comical dream.

The tulips giggle with bubblegum flair,
While daisies debate who's the fairest there.
Each petal whispers a pun or joke,
In this verdant realm where smiles evoke.

With mischievous weeds that twirl and sway,
They dance to the tunes of a grassy ballet.
Laughter echoes from leaf to flower,
In this wild garden, I find my power.

So come and wander, let light unwind,
In these crazy plots of the mind.
Let your spirits lift, leave woes behind,
In the whimsical gardens where laughter's kind.

The Allure of Aroma

In a kitchen filled with spice,
A whisk was dancing, oh so nice.
Garlic sizzles, onions tease,
Lemon zest brings me to my knees.

But then a cat jumps in my stew,
With whiskers twitching, oh what a view!
I sigh and laugh, what a great mix,
A meal with fur, now that's a fix!

A whiff of burnt toast fills the air,
A breakfast gone wrong, but who would care?
The toaster spat like it had a say,
I guess burnt offerings rule the day.

So here's to odors, good and bad,
Where chaos reigns, but I'm still glad.
For every scent brings joy or woe,
In my crazy kitchen, it's quite the show!

Momentary Whiffs

A breeze floats by, oh what's that scent?
A memory triggers, where time has went.
To cotton candy at the fair,
Where laughter echoes, and joy's in the air.

But wait, is that a sock I smell?
A mystery deep, I can't quite tell.
Is it the dog or the kid's old shoe?
I sniff again, and I think I knew!

Popcorn's popping, easy to find,
Each munch a giggle, joy intertwined.
Then suddenly, a whiff so grim,
What was that? Oh, it's just him!

So let us revel in quirky air,
With scents of laughter everywhere.
For every whiff tells tales anew,
In this humid life, we giggle too!

Fragrance of the Forest

In the forest, pine does call,
With acorns bouncing, nature's ball.
Mushrooms peek from leafy beds,
But watch your step, or you'll bump heads!

A skunk sprints by, a scent so bold,
That little dude with stories untold.
Flowers giggle, bees buzzing near,
But who knew nature hid such fear?

The squirrels chatter, let's have a feast,\nBut watch for nuts that never ceased.
A whiff of chaos, laughter too,
In this green world, I'm never blue!

So roam the woods, let scents do their play,
With each aroma, let humor sway.
For nature's perfume can make us grin,
In forests, funny thoughts begin!

Nostalgia in Bloom

In gardens where the daisies sway,
Old scents of childhood come out to play.
Bubblegum dreams float in the breeze,
With each sweet whiff, it's sure to please.

But wait, what's that? A veggie funk,
An old tomato, quite the junk!
Grandma's dinner, with roses near,
Where memories linger, bringing cheer.

A whiff of cookies, warm and bright,
Chocolate chips laughing, such delight!
But then a burn, oh gasp! Oh dear!
Guess that's what happens when you disappear!

So let the scents of life inspire,
With laughter and warmth, lift us higher.
In every bloom, a chuckle or two,
Nostalgia's fragrance, forever new!

Petals in the Breeze

Petals tumble, oh what a spree,
Dancing lightly, wild and free.
Bees are buzzing, lost in play,
Wishing they'd join in, come what may.

Laughter drifts on winds so sweet,
Silly squirrels, tap dancing feet.
While daisies gossip in the sun,
Who knew petals could be such fun!

The sun shines down, a golden hue,
Will the roses steal the shoe?
Tulips giggle with slight delay,
As springtime paints the world in play.

The Olfactory Journey

A whiff of onion, oh what a delight,
For pasta lovers, it feels just right.
Yet roses nearby poke their nose,
Saying, "Hey buddy, don't steal our pose!"

Cinnamon swirls like a pirouette,
While garlic rolls in, it's a brave bet.
Lilies laugh at the scents of spice,
"You think you're bold? How about this slice?"

Each scent a character, quite the cast,
In this nose ballet, it's a fast blast.
Get your noses ready, a smelly feast,
For every whiff might just invite the beast!

Essence of the Evening

The stars come out to sip some tea,
While crickets strum their symphony.
The roses sigh, all nice and plump,
As fireflies buzz, they're quite the jump!

Lavender dreams drift like a kite,
Then tumble down, what a silly sight!
The moon chuckles, it's quite a scene,
As shadows dance, all feeling keen.

Everything glows with a wink and a nudge,
Under this sky, there's no need to judge.
A serenade of scents takes flight,
In the essence of this joyous night.

Bouquet of Memories

A basket filled with echoes bright,
Of days long past, a pure delight.
Petunias whisper of summer's fling,
While sunflowers sway, making hearts sing.

Old potpourri brings back the past,
Memories linger, a fragrant cast.
A silly smell of burnt toast lingers,
While dandelions play, with their fingers.

Each bloom a tale, wrapped up in cheer,
Of winter's frost and the sun's warm beer.
In this bouquet, let's take a chance,
And twirl through memories, in a dance!

The Language of Blooms

In the garden of jest, blooms play,
Colorful whispers brightening the day.
Tulips tease with a twisty grin,
While daisies giggle as they begin.

Roses roll their eyes in cheer,
They tell corny jokes we all want to hear.
Sunflowers nod with a sunny sway,
While violets smirk in their quirky way.

Lilies whisper secrets so sweet,
Their perfume tickles, it can't be beat.
A pansy winks with a cheeky flair,
In this botanical circus, there's laughter to spare.

Elixirs of Calm

In pots of giggles, herbs conspire,
Peppermint grins, sparking a fire.
Lavender laughs, calming the scene,
While chamomile chuckles, all serene.

Basil tells tales of faraway lands,
With a dash of humor that truly expands.
Cilantro's snicker adds zest to the mix,
As their spicy banter pulls in the fix.

Thyme, oh thyme, takes a moment to ponder,
Before bursting into laughter, full of wonder.
In this herbal world, the flavors collide,
Leaving everyone chuckling, side by side.

Inhaled Harmony

Breath of blooms as laughter unfolds,
Tickles the senses with stories untold.
Jasmine sneezes, then giggles away,
While mint takes a sip of the botanical play.

Dandelions dance in a flurry of glee,
With each puffy puff, they're wild and free.
Breezes carry melodies soft and spry,
As daisies tumble and tumblefly high.

Inhale the humor, exhale the strife,
In the air of delight, we find our life.
Compose a symphony of petals so bright,
As laughter escapes into the endless night.

Petals and Poetry

Petals whisper rhymes as they sway,
In a bright ballet of fun and play.
Marigolds chuckle with colors so bold,
While poppies share tales that never grow old.

Daisies plot mischief under the sun,
Flirting with bees, oh what fun!
Forget-me-nots wink with a twinkling spark,
While zinnias bloom in the humor-filled park.

Tulips recite verses of curious twine,
With petals that tickle, oh how divine!
In this fragrant theater of color and cheer,
Every bloom has a punchline, crystal clear.

A Gathering of Aromas

In a garden, scents collide,
The roses giggle, petals wide.
A marigold's joke, under the sun,
'Why be serious? Have some fun!'

Lavender winks, with a teasing air,
While daisies dance without a care.
A whiff of mint, it joins the spree,
'I'm here, folks, who cares about tea?'

The basil grins, all dressed in green,
Says, 'Life's too short; let's keep it clean!'
With a hint of cheese, the herbs conspire,
To make us laugh, we'll never tire.

So blend these scents, let laughter flow,
In this garden where silliness grows.
Each aroma a note in a playful song,
Join the fun, smell it all day long!

Whirling in Blossoms

Petals twirl in a breezy dance,
The tulips giggle, given a chance.
Jasmine whispers, 'Hey, take a whiff!'
While dandelions puff up, feeling stiff.

The lilies laugh, their secrets they keep,
As bumblebees trip in a polleny leap.
Carnations chuckle, strutting about,
'Watch us bloom, turn that frown inside out!'

In this flower fest, jokes bloom like weeds,
While sunflowers share their silly deeds.
A merry bouquet, oh what a sight,
Making scents, bringing laughter and light.

Breathe in deep, let joy unfold,
While petals spin tales both bright and bold.
In each fragrance, a giggle is found,
In this whirl of blossoms, joy knows no bound!

The Sweetness of Solitude

In quiet nooks, scents come alive,
Vanilla giggles, 'Watch me thrive!'
With candles flickering, shadows sway,
Even solitude loves to play.

A hint of cocoa whispers soft,
'Forget your worries, let them loft!'
While cinnamon twirls in cozy ease,
Laughter wrapped in warm, sweet tease.

The air is thick with dreamy smells,
As gingerbread shares its sugar tales.
Lost in this sweet, aromatic space,
Where solitude wears a joyful face.

So find a corner, take a seat,
Let the scents of silliness be your treat.
In every silence, let laughter bloom,
In fragrant solitude, find your room!

Scented Illusions

A whiff of citrus, 'What's in the air?'
Lemons laugh, without a care.
Mint leaves frolic in recipes vast,
'Keeping you fresh, it's quite a blast!'

Romantic roses plot and scheme,
In a perfumed world, nothing's as it seems.
They whisper, 'Is it us or the breeze?
Sniff a little closer, if you please!'

Nuts and spices spin tales of delight,
Talking up passion every night.
Where cloves crack jokes and cumin sighs,
'Life's a feast, under scented skies!'

In this fragrant funhouse, scents play tricks,
Each aroma a clown, just for kicks.
So when you breathe, keep a grin in sight,
In scented illusions, all feels just right!

Whispering Lilies at Twilight

In the garden, lilies sway,
Chasing bugs that fly away.
They giggle when the moon peeks,
Sharing secrets, softly speaks.

Fashioned hats of petal flair,
A dewdrop's dance, a breezy hair.
They joke about the passing bees,
Who sip their drinks with graceful tease.

Whispers that the breeze can't hold,
Stories of the brave and bold.
At twilight's sneak, they laugh out loud,
Making magic in the shroud.

In their chaos, joy defined,
Colorful thoughts that intertwine.
With every chuckle, scent they share,
A symphony that's light as air.

Essence of a Dreamer's Delights

Dreamers wander, thoughts take flight,
With tangled tales through day and night.
In cozy corners, giggles play,
As whimsies dance, just bright array.

A sprinkle here, a dash of fun,
Tickling clouds, they run and run.
With laughter sweet as honeyed tea,
They sip the thrill of wild esprit.

Twirling visions, no one can see,
Colorful bursts of pure esprit.
Each fragrant humor, light and free,
As dreaming grows, so do we.

Through silly paths of starry gleam,
Dreamers live within their beam.
With every chuckle, worlds create,
And joys unfold while we await.

Bouquet of Untold Stories

In a vase of laughter bright,
Stories bloom in pure delight.
Each petal holds a tale or two,
Wrapped in joy, a lively view.

Down the hallway, blossoms race,
Competing scents in funny space.
Hints of mischief in the air,
Every bark, a bloom of flair.

Strange companions, leaves and stem,
Playing tricks, a witty gem.
Whispers of a time gone past,
In giggles they are unsurpassed.

Untold stories, one and all,
In this bouquet, they rise and fall.
With every wisp of air they share,
They craft a saga, bright and rare.

Aroma of a New Day

Morning yawns and stretches wide,
Spilling laughter far and wide.
Coffee brews in quirky cup,
Hopes and dreams are filling up.

Sunshine dances on the ground,
Jokes of shadows all around.
Silly birds with songs profound,
Awake the day with laughter sound.

Breezes carry whispers light,
Tickling leaves with pure delight.
Muffins rise with cheeky glee,
The day begins with harmony.

Every scent, a chuckle shared,
In this morning, none is scared.
With playful notes, the sun will play,
Aroma calls, come greet the day.

Scented Reveries

In a garden of giggles, I stroll,
Flowers whisper secrets, they extol.
A rose with a joke, full of charm,
Telling me tales, oh, how they disarm.

Tulips in tinsel, all dressed up,
Playing hide and seek with a pup.
Lemonade lilies, oh so sweet,
Offering laughter in summer's heat.

Pansies paint puns in hues so bright,
Chasing butterflies in pure delight.
With every sniff, a chuckle shared,
Nature's bouquet, humor declared.

So in this patch, let whimsy bloom,
Fragrant hilarity brightens the room.
A symphony of scents in the air,
Making us chuckle without a care.

The Allure of Blossoms

Daisy delights with a wink and a nod,
Sunflowers giggle, it's all rather odd.
Charming the bees with a whimsical tune,
Tickling the petals under a playful moon.

Lilies are pranks hiding in plain sight,
Bouncing in breezes, it feels so right.
A tulip tips its hat, so polite,
While marigolds dance in the moonlight.

Gardens hold comics, each bloom a jest,
Nature's giggles, they're simply the best.
With nature's bouquet, joy's in the air,
And laughter erupts from here to there.

Oh, flowers unite in a fragrant parade,
With petals of humor, they serenade.
In a field of giggles, freely we roam,
With scents of pure giggles, we make it our home.

Notes from Nature's Palette

A violet whispers a chuckle or two,
While daisies play dress-up in morning dew.
Lemons laugh loudly, quite tart and bold,
Offering puns in the marigold fold.

Breezes keep secrets, tickling tall grass,
As larkspur and lilac share tales as they pass.
A rose tries to rhyme but slips on its stem,
And the peonies join in with a laugh and a hem.

Nature's orchestra, so silly and sweet,
Each note a giggle, a rhythmic heartbeat.
Clover plays triangles, daisies clink glass,
A fragrant soirée where all the fun lasts.

So welcome this palette of scents and of cheer,
With blossoms composing the tunes we hold dear.
In this fragrant riddle, let laughter arise,
And dance with the blooms under bright sunny skies.

Fragrance of Dawn

In the dawn's early light, a fresh patter,
A blossom with humor, oh, how they scatter.
A tulip tells tales of the night's escapade,
While sunflowers grinning, in the sunlight wade.

The lilies out gossip, with whispers and grins,
Sharing their secrets about where love begins.
A daffodil chuckles, "Look at me sway!"
While the daisies laugh lightly, come out to play.

Mint leaves are giggling with every breeze,
Their fragrance a tickle, the bush of the trees.
In every petal, there's mischief in store,
Nature's own humor, who could ask for more?

With morning's soft laughter, our worries do fade,
In the perfume of dawn, new memories are made.
So toast to the blooms, raise a cup full of cheer,
In this garden of jest, there's nothing to fear.

Gentle Notes

In the garden where daisies dance,
A bee named Bob took a silly chance.
He sipped from roses, oh what a blunder,
Now he dreams of flowers, and under the thunder.

With petals like pillows, soft and round,
He bumbles and tumbles, never quite found.
His buzz is a giggle, a pollen parade,
In the laughter of blooms, his worries all fade.

Enchanted Scents

Oh, the lavender moon in a milky sky,
Makes fidgety frogs happily sigh.
They hop and they skip, with a scent like pie,
Plotting to bathe in the blueberry spry.

The mint leaves giggle, refreshing and bright,
While clumsy old crickets sing all night.
With every new whiff, the party grows wild,
In a whirl of sweet chaos, like days gone by, child.

Touched by Petals

Dandelions tickle the sneezing snails,
While flapping their sails, those pesky quails.
A ladybug laughed at a rose's big pout,
'Oh dear, you stink!' was what she let out.

With petals that flutter, and fragrances bold,
A bouquet of giggles, a sight to behold.
Through laughter and sneezes, they frolic and play,
In a world where we bloom, and fun leads the way.

Ethereal Aromas

In the haze of the morning, with a cinnamon breeze,
The gingerbread men giggle and tease.
Baking in sunshine, they're seeking their fame,
But be careful, dear friends, they're loaded with cream.

As thyme notes twirl with the garlic so bold,
The kitchen's a circus, a legend retold.
With each aromatic twist, laughter entwined,
A dance of delight in flavor defined.

Aromas of Serenity

In the garden, a flower sneezed,
It sent bees buzzing, slightly displeased.
A whiff of lavender floats on by,
Making the cats think they can fly.

Daisies giggle, violets tease,
Their scents blending like a soft breeze.
There's rosemary wearing a silly hat,
Thinking it's stylish, imagine that!

Petunias prance with a hint of flair,
While tulips dance without a care.
Each blossom whispers a quirky note,
Polishing petals, like a classy coat.

Laughter floats on the fragrant air,
In this floral chaos, none can compare.
With nature's perfume, life's a jest,
In this whimsical bloom, we're truly blessed.

Fragrant Pathways

Walking through the garden's maze,
I smell the pie that grandma made.
Basil's doing a little jig,
While mint plays tag, just too big!

A daffodil with a crooked grin,
Tries to battle with the wild wind.
Rosemary sings a funny song,
A melody where nothing's wrong.

Marigold's wearing bright yellow pants,
Swaying around, doing silly dances.
Sunflowers gossip about the sun,
As bees hold meetings, oh what fun!

In the garden, we are all friends,
With scents and laughs, joy never ends.
Each step is a giggle, each turn a sigh,
In this maze of smells, let your worries fly.

The Lure of Lilacs

Oh lilacs, you pranksters of spring,
Your perfume is a mischievous thing!
With petals so soft, you lure us near,
But your pollen makes me sneeze, oh dear!

Bumbling bees in a dance so wild,
Claiming lilacs make them feel like a child.
"Don't buzz so close!" cries a nearby fly,
As daisies snicker, oh me, oh my!

Hummingbirds dart, their wings a blur,
Drawn by the scent, they even purr.
A scent so sweet, it makes me laugh,
Jokes hidden within the green grass' path.

In lilac thickets, such whimsical fun,
Where the flowers paint smiles under the sun.
With every whiff, a giggle is born,
In this floral comedy, my heart is worn.

Whiff of Whimsy

A dash of mint, a sprinkle of thyme,
Together they tangle, oh what a crime!
Basil's busy plotting a new prank,
While cilantro's laughing in the back flank.

The daisies wear glitter, the roses wink,
Their floral gossip makes me rethink.
Who knew scents could carry such fun?
Skunks might run, but I just can't shun!

Poppies pretend, they play peek-a-boo,
With butterflies swaying, each one anew.
A chuckle escapes from the marigolds bright,
As the sun tickles leaves, what a delight!

In this patch of whimsy, we all delight,
With aromas that giggle, bloom day and night.
A fragrant adventure, we surely employ,
In this silly garden, it's purest joy!

The Secret Language of Flowers

Roses whisper sweet nothings,
Daisies giggle, oh so soft.
Tulips throw a dance party,
While sunflowers lean and cough.

Lilies share their best gossip,
As violets roll their eyes.
Pansies prank the bees for fun,
And petals burst with sighs.

Daffodils play hide and seek,
Waving from the garden's lane.
Carnations try to tell a joke,
But only bring about disdain.

Chrysanthemums throw a ball,
And everyone must wear a crown.
But beware of sneaky weeds,
Who'll try to steal the crown down!

Odes to Nature's Bouquet

In the meadow where flowers laugh,
The daisies wear a silly hat.
Buttercups play hopscotch, oh dear,
While ants march like a tiny brat.

Tulips sport a vibrant grin,
Gladiolas leap in the breeze.
Petunias gossip in bright hues,
While bumblebees tease with ease.

The violets tell corny jokes,
As marigolds blush with delight.
Cacti always join the fun,
Though they prick with all their might!

Dandelions float on giggles,
Spreading wishes far and wide.
But no one told the roses,
That they must also join the ride!

Perfumed Reveries

Scented dreams drift through the air,
As daisies chase the setting sun.
Lemon blooms make lemonade laughs,
And lilies frolic, just for fun.

Gardenia winks with playful flair,
While peonies twirl round and round.
Jasmine whispers, 'Let's be wild!'
And violets fall without a sound.

The petals clash in silly jest,
Competing for the softest hue.
While ferns try juggling with leaves,
And tulips giggle, 'Look at you!'

But watch out for a not-so-fun,
The dandelions' prankish winds.
They scatter laughs like pollen's dance,
Leaving us with giddy grins!

Blossom-Soaked Reflections

Echoes of laughter fill the air,
Hydrangeas chuckle by the path.
Mimosa trees wave their fans,
Inviting us to join their bath.

Roses blush at silly tales,
While orchids shake their heads in glee.
Sunflowers twirl in golden light,
And bid the clouds to join the spree.

Lilacs plot a garden race,
Carnations sport their wildest blooms.
Petals fly like paper planes,
Trading stories with the plumes.

At twilight's close, the garden sleeps,
With laughter echoing away.
For every blossom shares a joke,
Tomorrow's bloom shall have its say!

The Language of Blossoms

In gardens where the daisies chat,
Petunias giggle, just like a cat.
Roses gossip under the sun,
While tulips trade secrets just for fun.

A dandelion dreams of gold,
While pansies tell tales that have been told.
In a petal's whisper, laughter flows,
Oh, the jests that a flower knows!

Sunflowers tilt, with faces so bright,
Winking at bees with all of their might.
They dance in the breeze, a merry crew,
Making world's worries feel just like dew.

Oh, the blooms teach us with charms galore,
That life's too short to ever bore.
So let's join the blossoms, have a good laugh,
With blooms around, who needs a photograph?

Incense of the Heart

Burning sticks with scents so bold,
Whispers of stories waiting to be told.
Cinnamon and spice sink in the air,
But did you know? They tickle like hair!

The jasmine giggles, the sandalwood sighs,
While lavender pirouettes, oh what a prize!
As smoke weaves tales of love and mirth,
Even roses blush at their fragrant birth.

The heart feels lighter with incense nearby,
It's the aroma of laughter, just trust me, oh my!
A wisp of humor floats with a wink,
Let's dance with the scents, take a moment to think.

So light up a stick, and join in the fun,
With a puff of good humor, let your day run!
The fragrance of joy wafts near and far,
In the essence of life, we know who we are.

Sweet Perfume of Dusk

When the sun dips low, magic fills the air,
As night blooms blossom, without a care.
Whiffs of sweet nectar invite silly glee,
Where fireflies giggle and dance with the bees.

Lavender laughs as it dresses in gray,
Watching the sun slip away in the fray.
Petals close up, but their jokes remain,
Tickling the night with a soft, sweet refrain.

The moon grins down, a cheeky old chap,
In a floral disguise, maybe taking a nap.
With scents of the evening swirling about,
We twirl in the darkness, letting joy shout.

So let's embrace dusk with its fragrant delight,
In the sweet perfume of the soft starry night.
Where laughter and blooms waltz 'neath the skies,
An ode to the humor, where every heart flies.

Blooms Beneath the Stars

Under a sky with twinkling lights,
Daisies giggle, and so do the nights.
With laughter echoing from flower to star,
Who knew the daisies could play guitar?

A nightingale pipes, the daisies hum,
What a concert, oh so much fun!
With bees as the band, they sway and dance,
In the night's embrace, they take a chance.

Moonbeams sprinkle jokes with a glow,
As blossoms share tales in a whimsical show.
With petals as fans, and leaves in the mix,
Laughter blooms bright, like a playful fix.

So, join this party beneath the night sky,
With blooms as your pals, oh me, oh my!
In a field of giggles and fragrant cheer,
Life is a comedy when blossoms are near!

Whispers of Scented Dreams

In the garden, a cat does strut,
Chasing scents, with a comic strut.
A whiff of roses, he sneezes loud,
Leaves the flowers laughing, feeling proud.

A bee in a hat buzzes nearby,
Planning a dance, oh my, oh my!
With pollen in pockets, he takes a lead,
The flowers giggle, it's quite the deed.

A gnome on a bench, sipping tea,
Claims he can smell the whole wide sea.
But really it's just a hot dog stand,
And gum on his shoe, quite unplanned.

So here in this space, scents mingle and play,
Creating a symphony, funny and gay.
With laughter in petals, all crammed in seams,
The garden is buzzing with scented dreams.

Petals on the Breeze

Petals dance and whirl in the air,
A butterfly lands, a sight so rare.
But who knew the breeze had a playful twist?
Whispering secrets, no flower missed.

A daisy winks at a tulip bold,
"Bet you can't dance," the daring told.
They twirl in circles, all out of sync,
With giggles and petals, they clink and clink.

A snack-loving squirrel stops to stare,
Catching the scent of wild berry fare.
He grabs a petal, thinking it's sweet,
Ends up with pollen stuck to his feet.

A breeze so sprightly, with giggle and grin,
Turns moments of nature into a win.
With each fluttering petal, joy finds its squeeze,
Sharing laughter and love on the soft summer breeze.

Aroma of Forgotten Days

In an attic, dust dances in light,
Old roses bloom with a whimsical bite.
A musty old book, what treasures within?
A whiff of the past, let the laughter begin!

Sock puppets sing from the shadows, so bold,
Spouting sweet verses of stories retold.
They've gathered some dust, and a sprinkle of tears,
But their tunes rise up to tickle our ears.

A cinnamon jar, with a tale left behind,
Takes cookies and memories and mixes with time.
"Who knew Grandma's baking could cause such a mess?"

The aroma is rich, but it's chaos, no less!

Embrace all the scents of laughter and fun,
For every old moment is second to none.
Through the layers of time, let your spirit play,
In the aroma of fields from forgotten days.

Essence of Moonlit Gardens

Under the moon, the flowers conspire,
With dreams on their petals, they twist and retire.
The daisies are giggling, the lilies are wise,
In this garden of laughter, no need for disguise.

A hedgehog in shades struts with great flair,
Claiming the night as if it's his fair.
He moonwalks on ferns, quite the delight,
Challenging owls to a dance in the night.

The roses exchange jokes with the vindictive thyme,
"Your puns are so herbal! They should be in rhyme!"
Laughter erupts with a colorful glow,
As the stars join in with their twinkling show.

In the moonlit garden, scents swirl with glee,
Creating a ruckus for all to see.
Capturing moments with notes that outlast,
The essence of laughter, community cast.

Melodies of the Blossom

In the garden, bees do dance,
Sipping nectar at a glance.
Tulips sway with cheeky glee,
Whisper secrets, just for me.

A daffodil dons a silly hat,
While roses giggle, 'What of that?'
The daisies laugh in white array,
Telling jokes in the light of day.

Lilacs hum a tune so sweet,
With a melody, they skip a beat.
Forget-me-nots nod with delight,
Joking softly through the night.

Petunias plot with a cheeky grin,
While sunflowers boast, "We always win!"
In nature's bloom, we find our cheer,
With every laugh that we can hear.

Perfumed Reflections

In a flower shop, a quirky scent,
Roses mischief with present intent.
Violets snicker in blooms of blue,
"Why are daisies always in a queue?"

Sunflowers tease, "I stand so tall,
Why can't the tulips join the ball?"
A bouquet holds a secret grin,
Wrapping laughter from within.

Chrysanthemums wink, "Here's a tip,
If you trip, just let it rip!"
Jasmine jests, "What's in a name?
Call me pretty, I'll still be the same!"

In the chaos, scents perform,
Creating humor, a friendly swarm.
With every whiff, joy intertwines,
Sweet and funny, life aligns.

Ethereal Fragrance of Dawn

Morning broke with a zesty kick,
Lavender chuckled, "Take your pick!"
Dewdrops glimmer, sharing tales,
While gardenias ride on floral gales.

Citrus twirls with vibrant flair,
"Why are daisies always laid bare?"
The lilies chuckle, team in white,
They're striking poses in early light.

As sun peeks through with brilliant tease,
The marigolds giggle in gentle breeze.
"Do you smell that? It's giggle stew,
Steeping laughter, just for you!"

Petals flutter, whispers soar,
Nature's jesters, forevermore.
With each sunrise, a giddy start,
Sending joy straight to the heart.

In the Shadows of Scent

In the garden of giggles, scents collide,
Fragrant jesters take a ride.
Pansies laugh, "I'm quite the catch!"
While peonies sing, "No need to snatch!"

Under the moon, scent-friends unite,
Sharing puns in the cool, soft night.
"Ever noticed bees can't keep still?"
"Is it the sugar, or are they ill?"

Amongst the herbs, thyme steals the show,
With rosemary in tow, making it glow.
Mint's got jokes, a lively tease,
Creating breezes that aim to please.

In shadows where the spice does twist,
Funny aromas, they coexist.
With every sniff, we join the cheer,
In fragrant twilight, laughter's near.

The Essence of Heartstrings

A rose with a joke sat on my desk,
Its petals were bright, and it smelled like jest.
I tickled its stem, it laughed in delight,
In a garden of giggles, we bloomed overnight.

While daisies recited their riddle-filled rhymes,
The tulips threw shade, causing funny crimes.
With whispers of pollen, they danced in the air,
Holding secret meetings, a floral affair.

The lilies all giggled, their stories were tall,
Narrating grand tales of a dew-drop ball.
As orchids rolled on, with humor so slick,
They pranked all the cacti, made them quite sick.

In this garden of laughter, where joy takes the lead,
Each bloom tells a tale, it's a funny breed.
With heartstrings entwined in a whimsical way,
Nature's jesters at play, come join the bouquet!

The Scent of a Shimmering Tale

A dandelion dream wore a sparkly hat,
Telling stories of sparkles, of this and of that.
With windswept giggles, it danced on the breeze,
Announcing adventures with chuckles and wees!

A lilac came giggling, with a whimsical flair,
Sprinkling sweet scents like it just didn't care.
A giddy old jasmine joined in with a spin,
Their laughter erupted, where stories begin.

In a meadow of mischief, under sun's golden veil,
They conjured up wonders, each bloom told a tale.
With scents that enchanted and humor unwound,
A shimmering fable of joy would abound.

So here's to the blooms with their whimsical ways,
They spread joy like fragrance on bright sunny days.
In the garden of giggles, let's frolic and play,
For every new scent is a story in sway!

Whispers of Scent

A whiff of the daisies told secrets untold,
Of gnomes in disguise wearing jackets of gold.
With snickers and chuckles, the petals all spread,
Their echoing laughter would dance in your head.

The mint leaves were gossiping, fresh and so bright,
Sharing tales of the garden that bloomed every night.
With hints of vanilla, they conjured up cheer,
Telling jokes of the insects who patrolled the sphere.

A peony giggled, its fragrance a tease,
Sparking mirth in the breeze that tickled the trees.
With candied aromas, like sweets that delight,
The blooms spun their yarns under soft starlit night.

So lean in close, friends, to the whispers of scent,
For laughter and joy are here to prevent.
With every new visit to this fanciful show,
You'll find tales of humor in every sweet blow!

A Symphony of Aromas

In the garden of scents where the giggles collide,
A symphony echoed, with flowers as guide.
The lavender laughed and the roses would sing,
In a playful ballet, each petal a fling.

The marigolds swayed, with a funny little jig,
Their blooms creating patterns, all big and all big.
With a twist of the breeze, the daisies chimed in,
Conducting aromas where stories begin.

A garden of laughter, where fragrances play,
In a humorous waltz, as the sun burns away.
Each blossom a note in a whimsical spree,
Creating a melody, wild and free.

So let's twirl in the air, with our hearts full of glee,
In a symphony fragrant, where nature's carefree.
With scents blending sweetly, we'll dance through the day,
In this funny old garden, forever we'll stay!

Mystical Fragrance

In the garden, scents collide,
Lilies giggle, roses hide.
A whiff of cheese wafts near,
The neighbors punch in shock and cheer.

Jasmine jumps from vine to vine,
Swaying to an unseen line.
Dandelions roll on grass,
Wondering which ones will outclass.

Basil sneezes, thyme just grins,
Mint declares it's time for spins.
Petunias start a scented joke,
They laugh until the petals poke.

In this scent-filled, wild retreat,
Where each aroma has a seat.
With noses up, we dance and play,
Joyful in this bouquet ballet.

The Scented Muse

A pencil wearing a scent so grand,
Sketches out dreams just as planned.
Old spices sigh with tales to tell,
While pens and herbs form a sweet spell.

The citrus giggles, the cinnamon hums,
Building stories with aromatic thumbs.
Sugar plums sneak in with grace,
Swapping gossip in the fragrant space.

Vanilla whispers to chocolate bars,
Cracking jokes under twinkling stars.
With every whiff, a new tale pours,
They scribble laughter through open doors.

A world of scents in a poet's haze,
Creating flavors of hilarious ways.
In this joyful chaos of smell and rhyme,
The muse dances freely, lost in time.

Dreams in Bloom

A daisy spills its jokes on air,
While tulips gossip without a care.
Sunflowers laugh, reaching high,
Tickled by clouds as they float by.

In the meadow, dreams take flight,
With daisies under the soft moonlight.
A whiff of clover, sweet and bright,
Brings forth chuckles in the night.

Buttercups join in with cheer,
Tickling bees that buzz near.
They dance to tunes of breezy delight,
Sprinkling joy until it's bright.

So in these fields of blooms and fun,
Every scent feels like a pun.
A canvas of laughter and blooms galore,
Where fragrant dreams beg to explore.

The Aroma of Yesterday

Old cookies crumble, scents revive,
Whispers of laughter still survive.
Grandma's kitchen, warm and sweet,
Where every whiff is a playful treat.

Lemon zest and butter sigh,
Pie crusts tell stories on the fly.
Each aromatic trace we keep,
Turns memories into a fragrant heap.

From burnt toast to a cinnamon breeze,
Every wiff's a tease, if you please.
Like sock puppets, they dance around,
Whipping us up with joyful sound.

So here's to echoes, scents that flare,
Laughing as we linger and share.
With aromas of yesterdays so sly,
We'll savor the good times 'til we die.

Lush Reverberations

A garden whispers with a giggle,
Petals dance, they love to wiggle.
Bees tell jokes to the buzzing crew,
Even the roses are laughing too.

Lemons chuckle in their sunny zest,
While daisies play dress-up, looking their best.
A breeze carries tales from flower to flower,
Tickling the tulips, oh what a power!

The violets wear socks, a curious sight,
Dandelions are throwing a wild kite.
In this botanical circus, smiles abound,
The joy of nature, by laughter is found.

With laughter in bloom and colors so bright,
Each stem contains its own silly delight.
As bees blend a buzz with a playful tune,
This garden of giggles makes hearts swoon.

Unraveled in Bloom

An avocado slipped on a mighty green path,
While lilies snicker at the aftermath.
Petunias tickle the daisies awake,
This floral affair has no room for fake.

Sunflowers strut like they own the show,
Waving hello to all passing below.
A snapdragon speaks with a charming grin,
Telling the weeds they'll never win.

Tulips twirl like dancers in a line,
Determined to outshine the old grapevine.
In a world where blooms know how to jest,
Every petal seems on a laughter quest.

Pansies whisper secrets to each other,
Their jokes are better than any brother.
In the patch where colors comically blend,
Nature's humor finds a way to transcend.

The Mosaic of Scents

In the garden where aromas collide,
Lemons and mint take a goofy ride.
Chives wear hats made of fragrant leaves,
While lavender flirts, and humor weaves.

Basil giggles at the thyme's old joke,
Roses roll their eyes, but can't help poke.
Citrus bursts bubble like a fizzy song,
Each whiff is a chuckle, a laugh prolonged.

The clove sneezes, oh what a mess!
Fennel chuckles, in its own sweet dress.
Patchouli twirls in a silly embrace,
This scent playfulness fills up the space.

In the earthy laughter, meadows rejoice,
Every aroma has its whimsical voice.
Nature's bouquet mixes fun with delight,
Creating a tapestry, fragrant and bright.

Veil of Fragrance

Under a veil of delightful scents,
A daffodil wears pants, and that's immense.
The violets giggle in a soft ballet,
While a marigold jokes in a sunny way.

A lilac's a tease, very spry and slick,
Tickling the bees with a humorous trick.
Jasmine sneezes, the tulips all cheer,
Because every whiff brings laughter near.

Cinnamon rolls bounce from the spice shelf,
While herbs hold court, indulging themselves.
An otter made of petals breaks into a dance,
On this whimsical stage, they seize the chance.

With a waltz of aromas, they play with the sun,
Each scent tells a story that's bursting with fun.
In this fragrant realm, in merriment's clutch,
Nature concludes that laughter is such.

Notes of Nectar

In a world of sweet delight,
Honey bees take to flight,
Buzzing tunes, oh what a show,
Sticky fingers, don't you know?

Lemon drops and candy canes,
Jumping jacks in sugary lanes,
Lollipop trees that sway and spin,
Chasing dreams, let the fun begin!

Chocolate rivers flowing fast,
Giggling fish with fins that cast,
Whipped cream clouds that float so high,
Tickling toes as they fly by!

A sprinkle here, a laugh that trails,
Scented whispers carried by gales,
In this land of laugh and glee,
Sweet notes echo, wild and free!

Scented Soliloquies

Oh, the scent of burnt toast rings,
A morning choir of silly flings,
Pancakes flip with maple grace,
While catnip dances all over the place!

Bubbles of soap and lemon zest,
Giggles floating, we jest and jest,
Cupcake hiccups in the air,
Whiskered whispers, oh so rare!

Flavors fight like siblings do,
As mustard dreams and ketchup brew,
In the kitchen's swirling spree,
Smells compose their symphony!

A whiff of mischief, a dash of cheer,
As spritz of soda fills the sphere,
In this scented, lively play,
We laugh and dance the day away!

The Essence of Adventure

A whiff of popcorn in the night,
With chocolate dreams taking flight,
Slippers squeaking on the run,
Chasing cookies, oh what fun!

Jelly beans that hop and cheer,
In candy lands, we've no fear,
Bounce with joy on licorice roads,
Where every laugh like confetti explodes!

Bubblegum clouds in the sky,
Laughing ducks go drifting by,
Every scent a wild twist,
In this fragrant, wild mist!

So take a leap, dance in the breeze,
With every giggle, your heart will tease,
In this adventure, oh so sweet,
Life's aromas can't be beat!

Aromatic Portraits

In a frame of mint and lime,
Brush strokes dance in silly rhyme,
Canvas coated with a grin,
Art that tickles from within!

Gingerbread houses, gumdrop skies,
Lemons linger with sweet surprise,
Each color splashed with laughter bright,
Creating scents that feel just right!

Whirling twirls of cotton candy,
Sassy sprigs of herb, quite fancy,
Brushes, dipped in honey's hue,
Painting giggles, just for you!

So hang this piece upon the wall,
Where silly scents and dreams enthrall,
In every stroke, a giggle caught,
In aromatic love, we're sought!

The Fragrance of Memory

In the kitchen, pie once baked,
My nose recalls mistakes I've made.
A whiff of burnt crust fills the air,
Oh, how I wish I had a spare!

Grandma's cookies, a marshmallow goo,
They stuck together like a gooey crew.
Each bite a journey, sweet and round,
Now crumbs are scattered all around!

The scent of trouble lingers near,
With every laugh and scream I hear.
Battles fought with elder flower,
Who knew perfume could steal an hour?

So here's to memories we hold dear,
Where scents invoke both joy and cheer.
A dash of spice, a sprinkle of fun,
In scent, our stories are never done!

Serenade in Lavender Hues

In fields of purple, bees will dance,
With swirls of lavender, take a chance.
I twirl and spin with a silly grin,
While bumbling bees buzz all within.

The air's alive with breezy notes,
As butterflies wear tiny coats.
We laugh and stumble, what a sight,
With petals flying, pure delight!

Whiffs of lavender in my hair,
Smells like summer, can't help but stare.
What's that? A honey drop surprise?
I'd better watch out for those flies!

So let's embrace this fragrant jest,
With giggles wafting at our best.
In lavender dreams, we're free to roam,
And find laughter in a floral home!

Notes of Nature's Lullaby

Nature hums a joyful tune,
With notes of flowers dancing soon.
A chorus led by blooming trees,
While squirrels groove, hopping with ease.

The scent of grass, a tickle on toes,
As sunflowers sway, in comical rows.
A rustling breeze plays tricks with hair,
Oh, do we care? Not a single care!

Petunias whisper tales galore,
Of garden gnomes, they can't ignore.
A stinky cheese, whiffed from afar,
Spraying laughter, what a bizarre!

So listen close, to nature's song,
Where fragrant giggles can't go wrong.
In every petal, a secret's spun,
Let's laugh together, life's such fun!

In the Garden of Silken Scents

In gardens wild, a fragrant spree,
Where flowers giggle, oh so free.
The daisies prank each busy bee,
And roses blush, with glee and glee.

With every sniff, a tickle burst,
As petals flutter, quenching thirst.
A daffodil sings, 'I'm the best!'
While sunflowers jest, 'Forget the rest!'

The joys of blooms, a floral jest,
With tiny secrets, we're truly blessed.
A whiff of humor fills the day,
In petals bright, we dance and play!

So lift a laugh, let scents collide,
In this lively garden, let joy abide.
With fragrant twists, our hearts will cheer,
Creating memories year after year!

Tapestry of Scents

In a garden of smells, I prance and I twirl,
With a whiff of old cheese, and a new splash of pearl.
The flowers all giggle, as I catch their drift,
A bouquet of nonsense, it's quite the gift.

The roses are grumpy, they sniff and they pout,
While daisies keep dancing, there's no room for doubt.
Lavenders chuckle, with their sweet, syrupy tone,
But the thyme just can't stop, it's lost in its own zone.

Each perfume has secrets, that wink with a grin,
Like my potpourri stash, a wild, fragrant sin.
A sniff of the mint, and I suddenly leap,
But the onions I chopped make me wail and weep.

So here's to the scents, both silly and bright,
A journey of laughter, a spritz of delight.
With every new fragrance, there's chaos and cheer,
Join in the madness, let go of your fear!

The Poetry of Perfume

Spritz and spray, oh what a show,
I trip on a scent that tickles my toe.
A dab of cologne, but wait, what's that?
Smells like my uncle's old lost cat!

In the world of aromas, we dance and we flail,
With cherry blossom giggles and citrus that wail.
A perfume mishap, a sneeze, and I'm sold,
Hands in the air, too brave and too bold.

But lavender's laughter fills up the air,
While patches of moss roll without a care.
We blend and we clash, like socks on a spree,
Creating a story, as wild as can be.

So here's to our noses, our playful brigade,
Unraveling scents and the joy they parade.
With bubbles of laughter and unexpected wit,
Join in this poem, it's all quite a hit!

Embrace of the Earth

From earthy to sweet, oh what a delight,
Each smell in the air seems to dance in the light.
A mix of fresh rain, and a whiff of a shoe,
I contemplate life, while I smell my stew.

The grass whispers secrets, so soft and so sly,
While the mushrooms are plotting; I can hear them cry.
My sneakers are fragrant, a floral parade,
Even ants near my toes are crafting a raid.

Comic clouds float by with a perfume of fun,
Engaging the breeze, it winks with the sun.
A whiff of the dinner that's burning in air,
What might have been dinner's now just a dare!

But here in the chaos, my heart starts to sing,
Each scent tells a story, each note has a ring.
So lift up your noses, come join in the cheer,
For the embrace of the earth holds no room for fear!

Lush Whispers

In jungles of scent where the fragrance runs wild,
  A playful breeze teases, a mischievous child.
With a splash of cologne that goes out for a spin,
  And the roses complain with a chuckle and grin.

The coconut giggles, like waves on the shore,
While the lilac just sighs, it can't take it anymore.
  A mint on a mission, a basil that pranks,
  All conspire together and form fragrant ranks.

In a vat of confusion, I stumble and fall,
With an onion escapade that smells through it all.
  The lily confesses it can't stand the heat,
  But the fragrance of laughter can't be beat!

So raise your glass high to the scents that collide,
  With aromas that plot and fragrances wide.
In this lush little world, where humor unfurls,
  Silliness blooms; let's fragrance the swirls!

A Bouquet of Dreams

In a garden of wacky things,
The tulips dance and the chicken sings.
Petunias gossip, whispering loud,
While daisies wear hats, feeling proud.

Bumblebees buzz with a hint of sass,
Comparing pollen like a class.
Roses roll their eyes at the shoes,
While violets giggle at the news.

A silly breeze starts to play,
Tickling noses in a merry way.
Butterflies laugh in a fluttery race,
As sunflowers compete for the best face.

Every scent tells a goofy tale,
From garden gnomes to a big, blue whale.
So pick a bloom, give it a toss,
And let this bouquet show who's the boss!

The Aroma of Reminiscence

Nostalgia wafts like a burnt toast,
Bringing memories of dinner's host.
Grandma's stew with the secret spice,
Is a culinary game of Russian dice.

Onions cry and garlic sneezes,
Cooking woes are never easy breezes.
Her apron smells like a long-lost fight,
With scents of joy that feel just right.

Every sniff brings an awkward joke,
About burnt pies and a rusty cloak.
The fridge hums a sweet, quirky tune,
While leftovers dance underneath the moon.

So wherever you linger, just take a whiff,
Of laughter, mishaps, and grandma's gift.
Each aroma a reminder, silly and clear,
That laughter in kitchens is always near.

Secret Gardens of Scent

Hidden behind the garden gate,
Where daisies gossip on a playful date.
There's a lawn chair with secrets to share,
Where dandelions plot without a care.

A wise old fern with a top hat sings,
Of prickly cucumbers with ridiculous flings.
Sunflowers wear shades and sip iced tea,
Discussing the gossip of the bumblebee.

Each petal giggles, colors collide,
While the weeds throw a wild bumpy ride.
Every squirt of humor fills the air,
In a garden where laughter is everywhere.

So leap over tulips, embrace the delight,
In this secret place, silly and bright.
For joy is the fragrance, and we all want a shot,
In this magical kingdom where laughter is sought.

Hints of Lavender

A whiff of lavender makes me snicker,
Like a joke told by a friendly vicar.
It dances in air like a cotton candy,
Tickling noses, just a bit dandy.

In a pot where a cactus might bloom,
Lavender dreams without any gloom.
It twirls around with quirky flair,
As squirrels debate who's fluffiest there.

Let's sip on tea that smells like a breeze,
While baking muffins, oh what a tease!
Sneaky rosemary joins the affair,
Trying to smell sweet but having no care.

So sprinkle some humor in every sip,
With hints of lavender, take a trip.
For in this aroma, laughter is found,
In every whiff, giggles abound!

www.ingramcontent.com/pod-product-compliance
Lightning Source LLC
Chambersburg PA
CBHW051655160426
43209CB00004B/901